Who am I?

I am the vagina from Regina , my dad's name is Monty, and I am the milkman's daughter, you figure it out !

poetry

commentary

CELTICFROG PUBLISHING

This is who I am; my introduction!

Here I sit; this is it.

The things in my mind; may not be so kind.

I've witnessed a lot of things; sometimes hope needs a ring.

The kindness in my heart; shares a story that's so sharp.

The views I'm about to share with you;

Remember it's from my heart and my only view.

The first thing on my agenda; is the dope referendum.

Second ,thanks to Trump; well, that leaves us stumped.

Thirdly, our Army, I thank them; The Army, highly recommended.

The subjects I would like to touch;

Are meaningful, so I can't shut up.

It's my choice to share with all of you,

To give thanks, understand and question what is true.

I'm honored to say; I can write it in that special way.

The material in front of me;

Helps my mind to be free.

I have the gift of the gab, oh; I got that from my dad.

My mom taught me everything I know;

Look at my famous Lasagna; it sure steals the show!

We can't forget grandmas and grandpas; who loved to laugh and spoil us.

Now my brother and my sister; well, that's a new book soon here.

Back to my point,;
Trudeau just passed that joint.
Things about me; you will soon see.
You always knew when I was round;
I've turned your frown upside down.
I 've made you laugh or smile; you can see mine for a mile.
I always have great food around; and tell the best jokes in this town!
"Who am I ?"
"I'm The vagina from Regina, my dad's name is Monty, and I am the
Milkman's daughter, you figure it out."

This book is dedicated to the ones that love me!!
Photographs taken by Tom Pedrotti; one of my best buddies.

This is me, taking a break from gardening, on the first day of Fall 2017.

Table of contents

Part Two ... continued

It's time to remember the loss in November

Trash in a can

Wow 2021

Brush your fangs

The news sucks today

So much smoke and ash

One Year Later

Monte Lake Citizens let down today

British Columbia's worst floods yet

My final word is my favorite one

Part One

(A couple of recipes to share with the Army;
Because they enjoyed them very much!)
My famous Lasagna
Amazing Potato Salad

My famous Lasagna (serves 16-20 hungry people)

The meat sauce

1 tbsp oil

3 pounds extra lean ground beef

2 large onions, med dice

10 garlic cloves, grated

8 celery stalks, med dice

2 lg green pepper, med dice

2 lg red pepper, med dice

24 fresh whole mushrooms

2 can tomato paste

1/2 cup red wine or coffee

1 500 grams can of diced tomatoes

2-1.75 liter tomato sauce(any one of your favorite sauces)

6 tbsp beef bisto(optional, it helps to thicken sauce)

2 tsp cayenne pepper or dried chili flakes

3 tbsps onion powder

3 tbsps garlic powder

2 tsp ground cumin

1 tsp dry mustard or 1 tbsp squeeze mustard

2 tsp paprika

3 bay leaves

4 tbsp dried italian seasoning

1 tsp salt(taste sauce before adding any more salt)

1 tbsp pepper

2 tbsps balsamic vinegar(it help stabilize the acids in the tomatoes sauces)

I usually start by roasting the washed and dried whole mushrooms in an oven on 350 degrees, on a lined parchment paper cookie sheet. Drizzle oil on the mushrooms, a pinch of salt and cracked black pepper; or my favorite is Montreal steak spice as a substitute. Flip, after 10 minutes, watch small ones, another 5 minutes and they should be done. Take out of the oven and then grated two fresh garlic cloves on top at the end and try one, yummy! When cool, slice & dice and add it to the sauce after you add the tomato sauce. Or you could open up a can of mushrooms, drain water and add to sauce. For the sauce you will need a very large stock pot, drizzle the oil, brown the beef first with bay leaves, saute the onions, until tender on medium heat. All vegetables should be cut to a medium dice, now add the celery and peppers. Cook down for 15 to 20 minutes stirring constantly, add all the spices. After the meat becomes brown, add the tomato paste, turn down to medium heat and when the oils are starting to come out and things stick to the bottom of the pan deglaze with wine or coffee. This process will take a few minutes, when the wine is cooked down add the tomato sauce and bisto on top of sauce. Stir often, once heated thoroughly, turn down to low heat. Grate the garlic then add to sauce. Let simmer for at least one hour, while making the cream sauce for the middle layer.

The Cream Sauce

1 onion, fine dice

6 garlic cloves, grated

10 mushrooms (roast same as above)

1/8 tsp cayenne or 1 tsp red chili flakes (add more heat if you like heat)

1/2 cup white wine (the rest is for you while you sit and stir!)

1/2 cup butter

1/2 cup flour

2 cups chicken stock

2 block cream cheese,cut in cubes

2 cups whipping cream

200 grams grated parmesan cheese (it has to be the dry kraft brand, for texture and salt)

1 tbsp fresh finely chopped parsley

First I measure all ingredients and set up my cooking station. In a large saucepan, melt only a third of the butter, and saute onions, on low heat, with cayenne pepper or chili flakes, stir constantly, about 5 minutes, add the mushrooms with a little more butter. Sweat the mushrooms until all their moisture is gone, that is very important. Then add the grated garlic, add the rest of butter and flour, and cook the roux for a few more minutes. Cook on low until you can smell the nuttiness of the flour, about 3 to 5 minutes, careful not to burn. If this happens, deglaze the pan with the wine, this is when you add cream cheese. Cook the wine out before adding the stock first, in small amounts, add the stock, whisk vigorously, turn the heat to medium-high,you need to thicken the sauce before you add the whipping cream and parmesan cheese, make sure you whisk the entire time. After desired thickness, add fresh parsley, and turn off sauce. This should take 20 mins to come together, set aside. A must taste sauce; you can lick it off the spoon all day long. This thick sauce goes great with chicken or shellfish served on pasta.

The Healthy Filling

3 bunches fresh spinach or 1 large bag prewashed

2-500 grams ricotta or cottage cheese containers

200 grams fresh shredded parmesan

1 tbsp salt

2 tbsp pepper

2 tbsp balsamic vinegar

You will begin by cutting all the roots off, leaving part of the stems. Wash twice with cold water. Drain well or use a salad spinner, set aside. Mix the spinach and cheese, balsamic vinegar and salt and pepper in a large salad bowl, set aside.

2 boxes uncooked lasagna noodles and 900 grams of grated mozzarella cheese

You will need to cook the lasagna noodles al dente, as they will cook in the oven for 40 more minutes. Rinse with cold water or put hot noodles in a big bowl of ice, to stop the cooking process. Next grate the mozzarella cheese, set aside. Finely chop a good handful of fresh parsley for the garnish on top, and for your breath, lots of garlic in this lasagna. That's why it's so delicious.

Putting it all together

I build my lasagna in a turkey roaster. I suggest you do the same, at least use a 13 by 18 pan 4 inches deep. I then line the bottom with the noodles. We start with the ricotta mixture, spread evenly, and continue with the noodles. Press down as much as you can. I always overlap the noodles a bit each time and right to the edges, cut if necessary. Now we add a layer of meat sauce, at least an inch thick, (half the sauce), followed with another noodle layer. Here comes the lick it off the spoon all day, cheese sauce, spread evenly over, be sure to make it to all the edges. Then noodles again, the second layer of sauce, to follow with noodles. The final topping is 900grams of grated mozzarella cheese and some fresh parsley for garnish on top. Bake with lid on for 45 minutes (if cooking same day) until it starts to bubble on the sides, in a preheated oven at 350degrees fahrenheit. Remove lid and broil for a few minutes until desired doneness of cheese. Make sure to let rest a good half an hour before serving, or the cheese sauce will run out to the first corner you serve. Serve with fresh caesar salad and garlic toast. Just a precaution: your guest might want another piece to take home because they are too full to have another piece, right then, but would love another, so make sure you have enough! I usually make it in advance; as it can take a long time with preparation and cleaning up, thankfully you have some wine, a few noodles and a touch of the lick it off the spoon all day, cheese sauce left.

My Famous Lasagna

Amazing Potato salad

Amazing Potato Salad (serves 10 hungry people)
1 kg mini new potatoes
6 hard boiled eggs
3 celery stalks, finely chopped
4 garden fresh green onions, finely chopped
10 garden fresh radishes, finely chopped
1 tbsp garden fresh dill, finely chopped
3 dill pickles, finely chopped
3/4 cup miracle whip
1/2 cup mayonnaise
2 tbsp mustard
1 tbsp agave nectar or white sugar
1 tbsp salt
1 tbsp pepper
First off, wash and boil potatoes whole for about 20 minutes or until tender. Drain and set aside to cool. Next boil eggs for about 8 minutes, peel, wash and set aside to cool. Wash all vegetables and finely chop, as well as the dill. Mix all remaining ingredients in a separate bowl, to make the dressing. Cut the cooled potatoes in quarters, add the dice up the eggs, add the finely chopped vegetables, fresh dill and dressing. Mix thoroughly, cover with plastic wrap and refrigerate for an hour or two before serving.

05.16.2020 01:06

This photograph was taken on May 16th 2020 the day before the awful Snowbird Crashed right in front of my eyes, across my street. This Photograph was taken by Tom Pedrotti in the alley of McDonald Park, by The old McDonald Park pool, in Kamloops.

The Snowbird in the Sky

The Snowbird in the sky; I saw with my own eyes!!!

The noise in the air; I got up to stare.

Then a big squeal; like a semi lost a wheel.

Followed by a loud bang; like firecrackers going insane.

The man in the orange parachute; then landed on the roof.

As it never opened all the way; but in sight, two houses away.

The girl I never seen; as the next noise I screamed.

The plane did explode; before it hit the road.

It cleared all the trees; the power lines were all free.

The girl was not found; but later discovered on the ground.

Across my street; my heart did beat.

A crowd everywhere; suddenly everyone was scared.

The fire was out; without a doubt.

But the questions now asked?

With the Army and the police; now a Government task,

My heart goes out; and others no doubt,

To the Pilot we have lost; she gave her life at no cost.

Another tragedy close to home; now really burnt in stone.

May 17th will never be the same; the year that covid-19 came.

Everyone is close together; enjoying Kamloops weather.

Then all of this; I did witness it.

I'll never forget; the tears I wept .

Thank God no one else got hurt; it sure could have been worse.

Everyone was safe; now, let them solve their case.

May 17th 2020

This poem is dedicated to Captain Richard Mc Dougall and Captain Jennifer Casey

05.16.2020 01:06

This photograph was taken on May 16th 2020 the day before the awful Snowbird Crashed right in front of my eyes, across my street. This Photograph was taken by Tom Pedrotti in the alley of McDonald Park, by The old McDonald Park pool, in Kamloops.

Thoughts, after it hit me.

What I heard in the sky that day;

It was just before noon, on the 17th of May.

I was out for a smoke; staring at the sky for hope.

The next thing I know; the most horrific show.

The loud planes in the air; I wanted to get up to stare.

But by the time I would have gotten up;

It happened so fast I still had my full cup.

So loud, way too close; immediately, I knew it was something off course.

I shrugged my shoulders so tight;

I never slept for the next four nights.

So what no one saw; now I need to pause.

It happened right in front of me; I will tell you what I really did see.

After the first initial shock; I hear three pops, like thunder that rocks.

Then a loud piercing squeal; like a semi that lost its wheel.

Then a loud bang; not long after, things went insane.

The plane came into my view; it blew up, this is true.

An explosion at best: I'll tell you the rest.

Before it hit the ground; the parachutes blew out, with no sound.

Like a clown's magic handkerchief trick;

I saw the parachute hit the roof and the chimney made of brick!

The big explosion blew open a parachute; that's when I got off my stoop.

The girl I never did witness; as my neighbor's friend did help, just listen.

He jumped my fence; to perform CPR!!

But things were pretty intense in that backyard.

I'm sad to say we lost one of, "The Best;"

Bless her soul, as she did her quest!

She kept the plane pointed up to the sky;

So it wouldn't hit the neighborhood nearby.

The front end exploded in flight; with only the tail end in sight;

The end now first; as it hit the dirt.

A streak of flames ignited the asphalt;

Across the grass, to the front door, and then to a hault!

The tall tree, lit on fire; the smell, like a burnt tire.

Hydro was first there; climbing up the pole like a bear.

The plane missed the power lines; the people, the camper, the semi, and
The houses so fine.

Suddenly people in a chaotic freak show;

With a black truck blocking the road; "Driver, where did you go?"

The airport foam: it did perform.

By the time the fire hoses were hooked up.

The Army was there to set up.

The police had to use some force; to let the Army take its course.

I just have to say; the next day felt like doomsday.

So I had to tell my thoughts;

To the first officer, sorry, his name I forgot.

And the next thing I know; my Lasagna gives a good show.

The neighbors pitched in; our neighborhood did win.

Kudos, to the Army; also, thanks, for the Medal of Honor.

The way I look at it for me; cooking helped my mind be free.

And what I get out of this;

Life is sometimes forgotten and can be bliss.

I'm so thankful on one else got hurt;

We all need to appreciate God's dirt.`

Everyone has a story to tell.

So if you don't know me, my name is Michelle.

May 30 2020

This poem is dedicated to all the Snowbird Pilots; the Army, the Royal
Canadian Air Force the police and anyone who witnessed this horrible blast.

This photograph is a couple of patches from a couple of awesome Air Force guys, they ripped them off their uniforms and gave them to my awesome couple of kids.

This is the Medal of Honor, our family received from the Ministry of Defense for Canada, Minister Sajjan. We provided some meals and refreshments through the Covid 19 lock down, with the Army.

A different memory

Today was the very last day; the Army left on a nice day in May.

Kamloops will never forget; our community, it had some effect.

Again that plane; something so insane.But, with all
the right help; suddenly, the rain did   pelt.

The very next day it was like a ghost town;

With only the military and millions of ants on the ground.

The sky was calm, and the rain finally stopped;

With new reinforcements to help set up shop.

They were all here; as we held dear.

We need to do something; as they look for the wing.

Tim Hortons donuts and coffee; with no preparation, they had to flee.

No food, no tools; no drinks, and no stool.

So we asked if they would accept our gesture;

If we could cook, Lasagna, as it's the best here.

One General replied, " I just had a bagel, I'm full , but thanks."

I said, " Not now, it takes four or five hours, I think!"

Soon it was a yes; they will be impressed.

To get my mind off of this; Jennifer Casey we will miss.

We cooked it for our pleasure.

Sharing a wonderful meal; with the Army, a big deal.

Like a family so tight; with their bellies just right.

For a second or two; they forgot what they set out to do.

Thanks again, for your dedication; and for always saving our Nation.

I hope by reading this; we remember Jennifer, with a kiss.

May 20th 2020

This poem is dedicated to Captain Richard McDougall and Captain Jennifer Casey.

This photograph is the other side of our Medal Of Honor.

My mind wide open

The thoughts in my mind; this world so full of crime.

I've put many things on paper; sometimes I read later.

But now right in front of me; the best Military company.

The Army gave us a card; that I cannot disregard.

I love to share with you all of my weird views.

You may not like what I think; or what I say when I drink!

What I did witness in the sky; only gives me reasons to say, why?

I was always shy of my views;

But now I would really like to share my thoughts with all of you.

About all the crazy things that inspire me, too.

Like the refining of our oil, gas and gold;

That's killing our fish and polluting our seas;

Sends the rage in the sky, causing the destruction of our bees!

Let's talk about the people, what do we see;

By taxing all Canadians to save the refugees.

No offense, to the grateful people, they need our help;

But, what about the poor and the seniors and how they felt!

Put in the background; and no doctors to be found.

The teachers, treated unfairly; poor farmers no one, seems to care.

Here we sit; stuck in it.

With this covid-19 everywhere; "Where's Trudeau? Does he even care?"
With the discussions that are made;
It will affect the kids, who really want to play.
The First Nations and Refugees are good with you;
"F*** the white man, and pay your dues!"

May 20th 2020
This poem is dedicated to all those that care about our planet and the
creatures sharing it.

This world is nuts.

09.01.2020 02:31

September 1st 2020

This photograph was taken at the Kamloops Airport.

<u>My favorite one</u>

The last few days;...has been a daze;

With the sun shining with clouds of haze.

May 17th, the snowbird did crash;

Those memories will always last; as I'll never forget that horrific blast.

That day was to say, "Thanks;" for all the support from all the workers,

Working through this covid-19 time;

To give hope to all the people, who have also been affected by this world's

Horrible crime!

Some may lose their homes, dignity, benefits;

And many many pensions without friendships.

How will the government deal with this?

Many wonder and most just get pissed!

But, what I witnessed was like in an X-rated movie;

I really wish it was a naked boobie!

Back to my point.... Trudeau passed that joint!

He's too busy helping other countries;

What about our trees, that's not funny.

Expensive oil and gas; what Bill did you pass?

What do you care ... look at your hair !!

Bad discussions! Many repercussions!

Here nor there, the Army did care.

Cleaning up the mess; while you still get dressed!

No food,...just a Hotel ;... what the hell.

Not your problem; but we helped them.

My absolute pleasure; my family will treasure.

Kudos to the Army; they can be quite charming.

The biggest hearts; off the charts!!!

Thanks for all your dedication for saving our Nation;

Welcome to my house; like a special vacation.

May 21st 2020

This poem is dedicated to The Canadian Army, and the Royal Canadian Air Force.

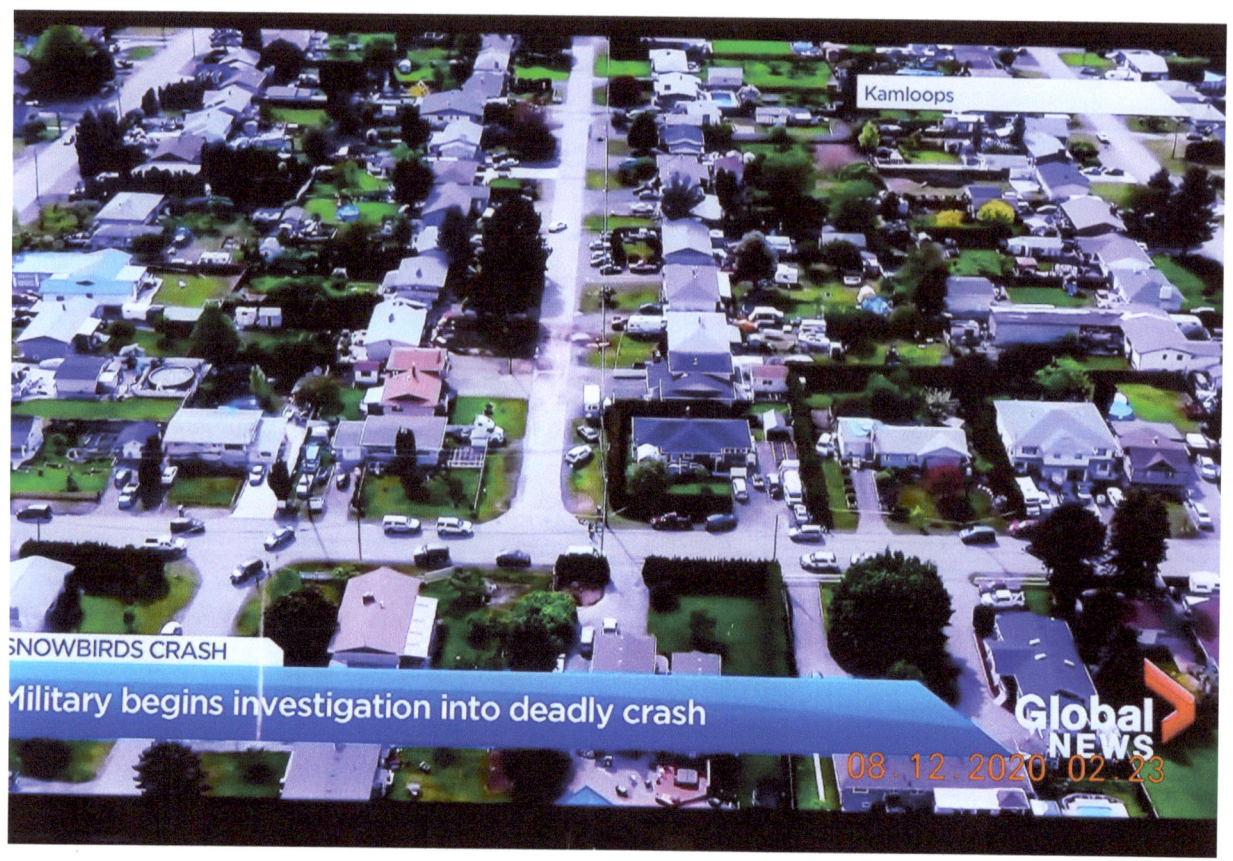

This photograph was taken off the TV; in one of these homes, there's me.

<u>What happened to McDonald Park Pool.</u>

At the McDonald Park Pool; the neighborhood was fooled.

Never a sign; they thought we were blind.

With things rattling off our shelves; everyone wondering, "What the hell!"

Our cars are all full of dust; some; silica and old must.

Yet, the water truck sat there all day; they never even got out to spray.

In fact, they never moved: until the end of their day!

What about our neighborhood garden?

"Ooops!"The Mayor might pardon.

" Environmentalists, where are you?";

Only a By-Law Officer, and what did he do?

He caused another problem; "Call the police, arrest him."

For hanging, then moving the sign, "SAVE OUR POOL!"

The excavator operator was kind, the By-Law officer, he's such a tool!

Enough about that; there is no turning back!!

The wind today; a huge dismay.

Now silica is in the air; no one does cares.

We lived with vibrations, loud noise; destruction, and poise.

Our Mayor did not stand; for this historical land.

He let them crush into the ground; and then laughed like a clown!

What the City Council might have known;

Now, burnt records can't be shown.

The land was donated by a man named, Angus McDonald;
For the children to play and act like good role models.
The volunteers of the North Shore community;
Built the pool for eternity.
Yet ,the records are gone, about how the community already saved;
Kamloops City Council was wrong, the North Shore had it made!
The community as a whole; all had a new goal.
To keep up, our settler's dream;
To have businesses safe and clean.
Soon after that, they rebuilt our bridge;
Which put new businesses out on a ridge.
The seniors got pickleball; the kids cried big and small.
The North Shore's community did change;
With all the new families in its range.
Now late at night, the City Council sleeps;
We will be filled with such a huge defeat!
The heart of the North Shore; will now be filled with new whores.
You have taken our favorite Watering Hole away,
Now, where will our new community go to play?
" In the Thompson River!!" I say!
The North Shore was the heart and the core;
Now, there is no pool to enjoy outdoor.

A Tournament Capital City; this is such a pity.

Now, where do the lifeguards take their lessons?

With this view, it's awfully depressing.

That's where our children first learned to swim;

While others enjoyed the sun and the wind.

This community has stood strong; never once did you listen to our song!

We were all too busy, playing at the park;

Meanwhile, you were ripping out our heart!

Just because City Council does not care;

We are still standing here to share.

All the memories of this; they will be truly missed.

Goodbye to McDonald Park Pool,

City Council, you're a fool!

For destroying our park;

So dogs can poop and bark!!!

April 17th 2016

This poem is dedicated to all the families that used McDonald Park Pool.

Also, to the families who built and fought for our pool to stay open!

09 11 2019 03 01

Parkcrest School burnt down today

I can't believe my kids school burnt today;

Especially, because it was only the third day!

Oh my, my, my; the smoke filled the sky.

Fire Truck sirens everywhere; the neighborhood was scared.

At Parkcrest School; the water did pool.

It was like a silence in the air; as many people came to stare.

Big pieces of ash fell by my pool;

We had to check it out, our friends lived next to the school.

My kids' faces suddenly just dropped; all that memorabilia is now lost!

The books, all that art; the gym, was the best part.

The lockers they had; as this is so sad.

The community will come together; as the memories last forever.

My heart goes out to all of you; what are the teachers supposed to do?

Whatever, we are dealt, please, do not Scream & Shout;

They will figure it out, I have no doubt.

Just be thankful no one got hurt;

A new school will provide work,

So let's not all panic; see what their plan is.

The resources are all there; we just all need to share.

Please everyone, be patient; useless emotions are now wasted!

Our community is strong; so our kids will get along.

Drastic changes will be made; for all the kids to learn, yet play.

As crazy as it is; we still have our kids!!

Thanks for listening to my rhyme; as things will get better with time.

To all the teachers and students; let's show them we can do this.

September 5th 2019

This poem is dedicated to all the staff and students at Park Crest School.

Written by Michelle Piluk; Monique and Monty's Mom!

These next three photographs were provided by the Fedoras, of the Parkcrest School burning down on September 5 2019.

Piluk's Creed To live by.

Always bake with good flour; hooray, for girl power.

Don't forget to wiggle it; and drink only a little bit.

Walk with a stride; keep your head high.

Never really boast; yet, be a good host.

Look around; write it down.

Always give others a smile; practice relaxing, for a while.

Regular showers; keeps super powers.

Clothes don't matter; recycle, that's better.

Elders are always first; with a great compliment burst.

Say please and thank you; so people won't spank you!

Be positive; like a relative.

Live creatively; and spontaneously.

Always remember births; as you were never first.

Being true to yourself; brings you good health.

Treasure your children; a family we build in.

Enjoy the weather; whatever your pleasure.

Look high and low; let your memories flow.

If you share; people will care.

Don't bellow about; give thanks, don't shout!

Food, don't waste; use toothpaste.

Always laugh; cuz life is a blast.

Universes united; stars will light it.

Take care of your body; so you can meet your hottie.

Give your children hope; please, don't smoke!

Keep your eyes on the road; don't text, you've been told.

Don't drink and drive; helps everyone stay alive.

Keep peace in the world; when you jump through your hurdle.

Listen with ease; never disagree.

Learn to let go of what you had; or your life will be mad.

The key to an easier life; is keeping a happy wife.

Love all your pets; clean up their mess.

Be humble, yet modest; that's what keeps you honest.

Love your house on the hill; be proud you are not Bill.

Travel to places; remember some faces.

Have no limits; discover what's in it!

Rhythm and rhyme; will flow with time.

Cook with love; flowers from above.

Stimulate your mind; grow something on a vine.

Look in the mirror; reflections keep dear.

Let's sing, let's dance; make true romance.

Kids are our joy; so put up with their noise!

Remember to lift with your knees;

Or your back will hurt when you sneeze.

Swings are fun; soak up the sun.
The circle of life; brings us peace at night.

January 10 2010
This poem is dedicated to Nichole, Courtney, and Leah.
They all had a say in this one!

04.21.2019 01.51

This Woody WoodPecker has a busy beak, with a surprisingly, watchful
eye.

12.08.2020 01.00

I wonder if your boss looks this happy on the clock; talk about the bird's eye view.

<u>Code of ethics at a workplace.</u>

When at a work site; smile and don't fight.

Remember a pat on the back; goes a long way, don't forget that.

Compliment and listen; the job will glisten.

When the work orders are at hand;

It doesn't happen with just one woman or man.

Everyone is equal; we learn and we give, we are people.

Do share your knowledge; if a problem, you can help solve it.

Work as a team; no need to scream!

Be proud of what you can do; instead of stealing that glue.

Let's all get to work; and not be that jerk!

So always remember safety is first;

No need for that shiny Hurst.

Have a great work day;

Oh yes, you will get paid!!

August 2nd 2019

This poem is dedicated to Thirsty Thursdays and Freaky Fridays.

<u>End Bullying</u>.

If you feel that it is wrong; then it might not belong.

It's ok to tell someone; so help, won't be long.

Acts of kindness; are near, not mindless.

Negative comments really hurt; so stop being that jerk!

Stop the pressure; and help him or her.

The more we give; the more we live.

Forget the chaos; come out, you won't be lost!!

February 4th 2016

This poem is dedicated to any one who was ever scared of telling the truth.

04.18.2019 23:06

Maybe we should act more like these caring birds; loving and more mature.

Another example of bullying.

The wrong that was done; was not even discussed to his mom.

The school staff sent the police; that poor kid, filled with such defeat.

The true story was never heard or told; how the kid was honest, yet bold.

He did the right thing; now he's in the spotlight, like bling!

He hasn't a hope; how will he cope?

A boy of nine; here's my rhyme.

We need to listen; stop all the dissin.

He was accused of a crime; that never crossed his mind.

Suddenly, at the stake; for another kid's mistake.

Let the story be told; the kid was returning the gold.

With rumors about; they point and they shout!

What is the lesson here? To tell the truth dear.

Apologies must be made; with some justice today.

If we let this go; bullying is the show.

How do we be a role model; when all people do, is squabble!

Pointing that finger...most of us have been there.

Please make it right; so he can sleep tonight.

February 4th 2016

This poem is dedicated to all the kids who have ever been bullied!

Those who are the bullies; infect people like a virus.

They need to be cured; and not heard.

04.11.2020 06:47

This poor goose can't figure out how to get loose.

He flew in there ok, but then; sat there half the day;

Feeling helpless, suddenly finding his will; then departing towards the Pulp Mill.

No matter the situation, don't be afraid; chin up it will all be ok!

Canada Day

Forget work, come to play; help celebrate Canada Day!

The weather was nice; with some beers on ice.

Popsicles by the pool; making the dogs drool.

Family and friends; reunited again!

Women and wine; men looking fine.

Kids will jump; slushies will pump.

Together tonight; fireworks in sight!

July 1 2019

This photograph was taken in the Westend of Kamloops; before Covid 19.

07.01.2019 09:45

It's time to remember the loss in November

" What is in their hand, "it's a gun;" I explained to the old man of 91.

Now it is 2018; this world is so mean.

With volcanoes erupting and some gasses in the air;

Do you know or really care?

We think of War;

Who really keeps score?

With all this political power;

Hatred controls the hour.

We forget who we have fought; never think what we sought.

This world is so corrupt; I think we've had enough.

It's time to remember; the loss in November.

For goodness sake; just bake a cake.

What will be tomorrow; regrets and many sorrows.

Now let's all save face; with peace and some grace.

Things need to change; cuz life is so insane.

So our children can live; and grow to give.

Let's all pray; for this today.

People need to see; without light, there will be no more Bee.

Time to reunite; we need peace insight.

Or, our story won't be told; about the music, Mars, and gold!

Let's figure it out; we need people to shout!

" Give up the Middle east and the Russian War; cuz people are already poor!!!"

November 12th 2018

This poem is dedicated to all Veterans and war families and the Armies, too.

This photograph was taken at Monte Lake before the wildfires of a Wild Clematis Flower.

Trash in a can.

Oh my, my mind was going; and for once, not so annoying.

We stood and listened; to all the things that glistened.

We love to share all of this; with our best friends and kids.

Let loose what we hold; I do think, is true gold.

Want to share it with them; so karma can now descend.

Take care of who we know; help families to show.

If strong minds are as one; bad will then be overcome.

Forget all the hate; not another mistake.

No matter fat or thin or the color of our skin;

We all have beating hearts within.

Be kind to yourself; share your wealth.

Just because the life we are in;

Doesn't mean you have to be bad to win!

Now, we smoke the dope; please, don't forget the Pope.

God made the burning bush; Donald Trump, and Purple Kush.

We need to take a stand; and not pollute our land.

Leave the fish in the seas; stop cutting down our trees.

We need flowers to bloom; so the bees can make their room.

Without slowing down our pace; we will have no more space.

The mountains want to erupt; cuz this planet is so corrupt.

The gods are all mad; their people are so sad.

They have nothing to do; but make slime from glue.

Like putty in their hands; who's in charge of our lands.

I thank all the First Nations and Pioneers; we should hold them dear.

Across every Coast; don't forget the Prairies, what good hosts.

Why the settlers stopped there; they got tired of all the Bears.

A good little joke; laugh or choke.

That's what we are forgetting here; the world needs a good little cheer.

Cuz life doesn't exist; without you and a kiss.

This once beautiful place; now becoming a huge disgrace.

Yet, we still have war; less sand on the shore.

The ice is now melting; and everyone is still pelting.

Stop raping Our Land; before there is no man.

Only Mars insight; soon there will be no light.

Then what will we do?

We got slime and no you.

" What do we need to do now?"

1 ,2,3,4,5, we have a crowd.

Being positive, using logic;

Hey, maybe we can solve it.

People need to discuss; this is all up to us.

To all the veterans; we should respect them.

What is our choice; for us, to use our voice.

It's time, the people take charge; with many we are large.

We are man; not mouse; come on, use your mouth.

Fight for our rights; so we can have peace tonight.

January 21th 2019

01.21.2019 05:55

This is McDonald Park on January 21 2019 of the Moon.

Wow 2021

It is now 2021; what has this world really become?

With now Trump out of hand; the Army, here we go again!

Trudeau, " What does he know?"

Senate on vacation, "Where did they go?"

New vaccination on demand; now covid-19 flooding, Our Land.

The Government should now take a stand;

To destroy It or fight for It, what's the Command?

Give us some hope; cuz, no one can cope.

The Land is Our Own; soon no one will roam!

With a miracle; this is curable.

"What is this?"... Leave it to cheese whiz!!!

The US has gone mad; with Trump so Bad.

The Riots, Trump had caused; made everyone pause.

Now, Biden on hand; talking about a changed man.

The day of Inauguration; Informs, the nation.

What kind of man will he be?

That's for eyes to see.

January 20th 2021

Brush your fangs

Brush your fangs; brush your fangs; Say to plaque, " No More!"

Brush your fangs; brush your fangs; brush your fangs some more.

Up and down; up and down; no cavities no more!

Up and down; up and down; brush your fangs some more.

Back and forth; back and forth; don't forget your crowns!

Back and forth; back and forth; brush your fangs some more.

Rinse your mouth; rinse your mouth; and spit it in the sink!

Rinse your mouth; rinse your mouth; rinse your mouth once more.

Wash your face; wash your face; till you see no more toothpaste!

Dry your hands; dry your face; and don't forget to wipe the sink!

January 2012

This poem gives us something to smile about and show off our fangs.

The next two photographs are of our magical moon; at McDonald Park

01.20.2019 08:48

01.20.2019 09:57

The news sucks today.

Our world today with our government; what do I say.

Thanks to the government; we all need to pray.

The lies and the deceit; they have us all beat.

With some corruption to our faith;

We thought freedom was so great.

Stuck indoors;

Looking at the scores.

People we care about;

No hugs, we can only shout.

What about that poor child?

Such racism is running wild!

But now all we have is a new virus;

Yet, no one has been punished for infecting us.

We are just kept in the dark;

Like a growing mushroom, that smells like farts!!!

Only the rich will survive;

Hoping for that Canadian Pride.

All I have to share; people are f**k**g scared.

Feeling hopeless all the time;

Especially when Covid takes someone so kind.

February 17th 2021

This poem is dedicated to a friend who lost a few loved ones from the Covid 19 virus.

So much smoke and ash

The glistening streetlights capture the falling ash;

The red Moon, the red Sun, you can only see, in a flash. Some days the smoke is so low in our Valley;

When you hit your golf ball, you can't even see it going over that gulley. We may not be able to go outside to play;

But just think of Lytton, how it burned away! With the heat wave and loud lightning strikes;

The hottest ever, you couldn't sleep in the night.

Over a thousand fires since the 1st of April 2021;

Burning BC, now Alberta, Saskatchewan;

Canada what have we done?

People and the Gods, whatever it may be;

We need to be more respectful, keep your smokes where you can see. Put out your fires; even if you're tired.

Now other countries are lending us a hand;

Most of them are tenting out, you should see it, oh man.

Red ones, yellow ones, purple ones, green ones, and blue ones; Like a box of Smarties, yet the courageous ones!

The Fireweed; was help indeed.

Where my children's School already burnt to the ground;

They are fed, with trailers, shower facilities, and a place to cool down.

I just want to say thanks to all the Firefighters for their efforts; Using great skill, with tons of smoke, they work hard under pressure.

With 275 fires still burning for miles; Look at the people, they lost their smiles.

They lost their land and their hope; How will they really cope?

My heart goes out to you;

The government will pay their dues. The Canadian Red Cross is the best;

After their visit you can finally get rest!

August 2021

This poem is dedicated to all the folk that lost everything including their dignity in all those horrible fires.

One year later

One year later we reflect on the crash.

As I will never forget that horrific blast.

The community is still healing;

The house that it hit, still in the dealing.

With everyone reminded on this very day;

While others think about it day to day.

But here nor there...Kamloops does care!

Jennifer Casey is so sadly missed.

Now, the community has a new twist.

A bench at the airport;

We can now sit long or short.

To reflect what is truly dear;

Anyone can enjoy and sit here.

In memory of Jennifer Casey;

A wonderfully charming beautiful Lady.

May 17 2021

This poem is dedicated to anyone who ever met Jennifer Casey.

The Monte Lake Citizens got let down today

The fires this year; destroyed families so dear.

The record heat this summer; caused so many fires, in number.

All the water was there; but, there was no help to care.

Out at Monte Lake in particular;

Not everyone was notified to, "Get the heck out of there!"

" Help is on its way;"

They were fooled that day.

Them lying again; saves them money, in the end.

Some with insurance; others need reassurance.

They pay taxes; "That's the facts!"

Now, the only people that stuck around to fight;

Was the neighbours close by, they stayed up all 3 nights.

Not one person came around; to help fight fires, all over their ground.

It was briefly on the news;

"What are the citizens going to do?"

They only end up in a stack of papers, on a desk;

Waiting for someone to process them, the neighbors say,

"What the heck!"

Again lost in the dust; the Mayor won't discuss.
My friends dad's house and property burnt to the ground;
All his 90 year old parents things, nowhere to be found.
I guess they weren't important,
They didn't mean a thing.
Not even an animal, or a bird to sing.
Now he is laid to rest; his land sits in such a mess.

July
This poem is dedicated to Jim and Petronilla Pedrotti and all the folks
who lost anything in a fire.

The next three photographs are of Jim's Property and house at Monte Lake.

British Columbia's worst floods yet

So many floods these past years; brings folks to only tears.

Especially this past year it was the worst;

It could have been prevented, that's what hurts.

Especially down on the Vancouver coast;

Now the politicians hide like ghosts!

They were told by the farmers to fix up their dykes;

Or, we will have floods and ALL our food goes up in price!!

Why are our voices not heard?

Environmentalists, they are perturbed.

We need our government to listen;

Nevermind all the excuses and you're dissin.

" Not enough money to go around;"

As Trudeau runs us to the ground!

How do we fix a political mistake?

Only the taxpayers are at the stake.

All the highways now crumbling;

The whole Province is just grumbling.

With massive amounts of rain;

Now the town of Princeton has gone insane.

" Please help us clean up our land!"

The citizens asked the Army to command.

Merritt got hit on both accounts;
Remember the logging, "Do a TREE count!!!!!!!!!!"
Our Province, now flooding; climate change, not changing.
The heat caused many fires;
Remember LYTTON, now, no houses to see.
Jessica Lightfoot, mayor, I had a chance to know;
I hope things are alright, you're a good show!
Things need to change; keep our Resources in range.
So we don't have to repeat this again;
It's too much, people will go insane.
Another way to look at it; when your highways changed a little bit,
You explore new valleys, you've never seen before.
If ever in Hedley, you must stop at the store.
The History there will blow your mind;
Also "The Bratt's Pizza", is one of a kind.

February 15 2022
This poem is dedicated to the folks of the Similkameen Valley; from the
Gold Dust Pub, hello from Miss. Gold Dust!

My last word is always my favorite one

This world and its crime; we should stop and rewind.

The view I have; people might be glad.

For I am about to speak; about a passion so deep.

The Universe as we know it;

Soon won't be so iridescent!

The FIRES, the FLOODS; the sliding mountains of sludge.

Now everyone is involved;

Will the Government help solve?

How stupid we are; we have come so far.

To pollute this Earth; who wants to rebirth?

The doctors are mad; with Covid so bad.

It makes it very hard to cope;

Remember the mudslide in Hope?

With our healthcare on stand;

Yet, no one is leading a hand!

Our government helps all of our guests;

The tax paying citizens lay them to rest.

They can't get the help;

Guess how they felt!

Corrupt as a nation; Trudeau the creation?

What we believe; no one can perceive.

False hope; look at the Pope.

What does everyone make of this;

The First Nation children, that's what really got missed!

Why are we so dumb;

Justice needs to be done.

The knowledge was there; but no one really did care.

Now finally the truth;

About the FORGOTTEN YOUTH!

Let's take a pause;....

... Now what does this cause?

A covered up matter;

With bodies so scattered.

Our faith is at stake;

The Catholics, a mistake?

Is the government to blame?

Who hid all their shame?

Some people did know;
But NEVER talked about the show.
They kept it all inside;
Some forgot, or left;
While others went to hide.
Now the truth be told;
Some land was now sold.
The government is to blame;
People hold their heads in shame.
You know who you are;
As karma is not very far.
It will all come out in the wash;
About the loved ones we all lost.
No matter, fat or thin;
Or, the color of our skin.
Justice will be made; and taxpayers will pay.
Trudeau will sit strong; the rest won't get along.
We need to change our thoughts; so our values can mean a lot.
Back to our Earth;
What is it worth?

Life as we know;

Soon won't grow.

With the sadness in the air; still the right people don't care.

The rich will exist; the poor, out the door.

The middle class; can kiss his ass!

They go to work; without a perk.

No healthcare soon around;

Trudeau ran that to the ground.

No pensions perhaps later;

Just an Aspirator.

What that means; we're stuck in between.

In three years, Canada will be bankrupt;

'' Trudeau, Cheers!'' now we are going to be f***ed!!

October 26 2021

Dedicated to all the families who ever lost a child because of their race; that does not mean they needed to be erased!!!

Who am I ? Part Two

I am Monty's dirty dirt's daughter; Box up Price down.

Are you ready for round two?

Thanks for reading. I hope you all enjoyed it and found

some release in any way, I know it helped me.

michellepiluk@gmail.com